# CONVERSATE:

Discussion Questions Inspired by the Black Experience

*3rd Edition*

Odogwu O. Linton, Esq.

*© 2014, 2020 Odogwu O. Linton, Esq. All Rights Reserved.*

© 2014, 2020 by O. Linton.   All rights reserved.

No one associated with the development or publishing of this book assumes any responsibility whatsoever for any direct or indirect damage or injury to any person or property associated with the reading, discussion or use of this book or its contents.

No part of this book may be reproduced, stored in a retrieval system or transmitted by any means, electronic, mechanical, photocopying, recording or otherwise, without prior, written permission from the author.

All product names and brands are property of their respective owners. All company, product and service names used in this book are for identification purposes only. Use of these names and brands does not imply endorsement or ownership.

**ISBN:** 9798652019150

© 2014, 2020 Odogwu O. Linton, Esq.   All Rights Reserved.

# Introduction

> "If a race has no history,
> it has no worthwhile tradition,
> it becomes a negligible factor
> in the thought of the world,
> and it stands in danger of
> being exterminated. "
> - *Carter G. Woodson*
> Negro History Week, P. 29

I am pleased to welcome you to the 3rd Edition in the *Conversate* series, updated for today's times.

Written originally as a conversation starter, *Conversate* invites you into a sliver of the daily-shared experience of Black Americans, through the most basic way possible, and within the comfort of your own space. Within these pages, you will expand your understanding of the Black experience by simply answering questions posed in a Socratic Method style. While there are a few surprises, there is no correct pattern to follow, no secret to break. Pick any number, flip back

© 2014, 2020 Odogwu O. Linton, Esq.   All Rights Reserved.

and forth, just begin. You will learn a little more about yourself with every question answered. Some would seem generic, but all are written specifically and precisely to allow you, the reader, to explore issues related to the Black experience.

One word of caution: Prepare yourself for an experience unlike any other. The questions are provocative and challenging. After watching hundreds of people explore these questions in formal and informal settings, and receiving feedback from many more, it is clear that this book will change your way of thinking about yourself and your friends.

If you are honest and reflective, it will take you days, maybe weeks to complete the entire book. You will laugh, you will cry, you will skip some out of frustration and will be humbled by questions that challenge your very understanding of yourself and the world we all share.

And that's if you answer the questions on your own.

© 2014, 2020 Odogwu O. Linton, Esq.  All Rights Reserved.

Should you explore the questions with friends or family, be prepared to meet, for the first time, people you thought you knew.

Allow me, therefore to introduce you - to yourself.

**Go ahead, and**

## *Conversate!*

© 2014, 2020 Odogwu O. Linton, Esq.   All Rights Reserved.

## **DISCLAIMER**

The publisher, author, his affiliates and assigns assume no liability for any harm or injury that results from the use of this book or its contents.

As the reader, you assume all responsibility for any experience that results during and after reviewing these questions.

© 2014, 2020 Odogwu O. Linton, Esq.   All Rights Reserved.

1

Your friend tells you that she was called to her daughter's school by the Principal.   The Principal says the daughter was so angry about her grades that she dabbed on the teacher and stormed out of the classroom.  Your friend asks you for advice.

What do you say?

2

Do you know anyone who has a "system" to play the lottery?

Do they win?

3

Late one evening, you are waiting in a parking garage by yourself for a very slow elevator. When it finally arrives, you go in. While the doors are still open and before you push a button for your floor, four Black men hurry into the elevator with you.

The doors are about to close.

What do you do?

4

What should a politician do to earn your support on Election Day?

5

After leaving her husband, your Aunt and her four children move down the street from you. She takes a job and expects you to help her out by watching her children a few times a week.　She never mentions paying you.

What would you do?

## 6

Your friend Anton wins ten tickets to a comedy show.  Your friend Renee does not want to go because the seats are in the front row and since she is overweight, she is concerned the comedians will crack jokes on her.  She says she will go only if you sit next to her.

Will you go?

7

Your niece is going to get her first driver's license.  She asks for your advice regarding applying to become an organ donor.

What would you tell her?

## 8

Your Black friend's 12-year-old daughter is missing. It has been 15 hours and no one has heard anything.

Would you expect the local media to cover the story?

9

You see your son's friends running down the street, followed by several police officers. You later overhear your son talking to his friends.  They all got away.  The next day, the police are going door to door passing out fliers looking for them.

When the police come to your door and ask you if you will help them find your son's friends, what will you say?

# 10

## Should African Americans have independent representation in the United Nations?

## 11

Under what conditions, if any, would you lend a family member a large sum of money?

## 12

Your Uncle Joe comes home with a big smile on his face. When you ask why he's so happy, he says a woman told him he's a "Good Black Man".

What would a man have to do for you to tell him the same thing?

13

While watching a movie in a theater, the person sitting in front of you begins talking on the phone.   The movie's about to start.

What will you do?

## 14

Your friend tells you that he and some of his friends are eager to attend a rally in support of reopening the economy after the COVID 19 quarantine.   Since the rally will be in an "open carry" state, they will be wearing fatigues, military gear and are taking their assault rifles with them.

Five of your Black friends, who are barbers and hair stylists, want to go too, but they are concerned about taking weapons.   They ask for your advice.

What would you tell them?

15

You get a call from your Aunt.   She's at a mall, asking that you drive 25 miles to pick her up because she doesn't have enough money to get home.

What would you do?

16

You see a person back into your car, leaving a small dent in the door.   The person does not leave a note and does not know it is your car.  They drive off before you can confront them.  Later at an evening event, you see the same person.

What would you do?

# 17

## Do you believe God wants you to tithe?

## 18

Do you believe the LGBTQ equality movement is comparable to the US Black Civil Rights movement?

## 19

Do you consider Africa your "father or motherland"?

20

Your romantic friend of several months wants to get serious in your relationship, but your family wants you to end it.

What would you do?

# 21

What characteristics did former United States President William Jefferson Clinton exhibit for some to call him America's "First Black President"?

22

Your friend is nervous about meeting his girlfriend's parents.   One is Black, the other is not.

What advice would you give your friend?

23

Do you have any friends or family members that refuse to get a job?

24

If you saw someone shoplifting in your favorite store, would you alert the store security?

25

While out with friends, a person not of the sexual persuasion you prefer asks you out with clear romantic intentions.

How would you respond?

26

Do you believe that racial profiling occurs?

27

Who is the most prominent Black leader in America today?

Why?

**28**

Your friends know three people that are interested in dating you.   One has poor credit; the second still lives at home and the third has two young children.

Are you going out?   With whom?

## 29

What impact did the COVID – 19 quarantine have on your friend and personal relationships?

30

Do "successful" Black people have an obligation to "give back" to the Black community?

## 31

Do you give money to beggars?

32

Does the United States government have an obligation, moral duty or legal mandate to give either reparations or an apology to Black people whose ancestors were forced to work as slaves in the United States and/or its territories?

## 33

Your friends know three people that are interested in dating you.   One has a very high profile, public career; the second travels frequently; and third is financially stable, but is involved with several other people that are interested in a relationship.

Are you going out?   With whom?

## 34

What actions would the Federal government need to take to satisfy a mandate to give reparations to Black people?

35

Do you own any original African clothing?

## 36

You see your friend's husband at a restaurant in an intimate embrace with another man. Later, when you confront him about this, he claims that he is not interested in other men, but he occasionally likes to spend intimate time with them.   He then asks you not to interfere.   You know that your friend (his wife) has no idea this is occurring.

What do you do?

## 37

You get invited to participate in a new African dance exercise class in a local gym.   When you get there, you find out that the trainer has never been to any African country.   When the class starts, the trainer comes out dressed in outrageous attire that you know is not from any African country.   As part of the routine, the trainer jumps around babbling and chanting.

How would you respond?

## 38

What is your go to app when you are bored?
When did you last play?

39

A website offers you a gift worth $100 if you provide the email addresses of ten friends.

Will you provide the emails, or pass on the gift?

## 40

You are surprised to learn that a close friend is secretly abusing drugs.

What would you do?

## 41

While waiting at a bus stop, a young pregnant woman with four young children begins complaining loudly that the government's financial assistance is not enough for her to live comfortably.

She asks you what she should do.

What would you say?

## 42

Your friend's grandmother proudly shows you pictures from her vacation on her new cell phone.  She then asks if she can see your phone so she can see some of your favorite pictures.

What would you do?

## 43

You have won a free dinner to your favorite soul food restaurant. With plate in hand, you get to choose from the open buffet. All of the best-known selections are there, waiting for you!

Everything's ready— what do you pick?

## 44

Name the top three types of businesses found in Black communities.

45

Did you have domestic chores in your home when you were a child?

What did you have to do?

46

You arrive at an event where there is only one Black person in attendance.

Would you make an effort to meet that person? Why?

## 47

Your friend's nephew has been accepted at two colleges, one a HBCU and the other the State's large, official university.  He is not sure what career he wants to pursue, but he does want a good education and wants to be well prepared for life afterwards.

Which school would you recommend he attend?

## 48

Do you shop more than usual on Black Friday?

Are you first in line, or first online, to get an advertised sale price?

49

What advice would you give to someone that has been a victim of domestic violence?

If the abuse occurred in front of you, would you intervene?

## 50

While waiting in line at a store, you overhear a local high school sports coach discussing a student athlete's intention to drop out of high school to play professional sports. The coach notices that you heard the conversation, and then asks what you think he should say to the student.

What would you advise the coach to do?

## 51

There are many reality TV shows, but if there was a show about THIS, I know everyone would watch.

Describe the show.

## 52

If you were a single parent looking to get married, what standards must a person meet before you introduce them to your children?

## 53

While standing in line at a store, you overhear a person talking on the phone about an advertisement seeking African Americans to test an experimental drug. Participants may receive a small payment for participating.

Will you sign up?

## 54

There are over 50 countries in Africa. How many can you name?

Just how many countries *are* in Africa?

55

Are you or a family member active in any historically Black organizations?  Do you believe they provide a valuable service to the Black community?

## 56

If you could choose to live the life and experience of any Black character from a television show, which would you choose?

What life would you choose for your youngest relative?

## 57

While out with a group of friends, you decide to go to a fast food restaurant. One of your friends recommends a certain restaurant, claiming that a friend who is a new employee will "hook everyone up".

Will you go and eat for free?

## 58

## Are Black people better off today than fifty years ago?

## 59

While waiting to be seated in a restaurant, an elderly Black couple sits nearby. You overhear them say that they have been married for over 40 years and have many children and grandchildren. As you get up to go to your seat, another waiting couple asks them for the secret to their happy marriage.

Unfortunately, you do not hear the answer.

What do you think they said?

## 60

Say your favorite line from a movie. Why is that your favorite?

## 61

You are a member of an organization that advocates on behalf of Black causes.  When the time comes to choose a new leader, a White person enters the election and asks for your support.

Would you give it?

# 62

# Do All Lives Matter?

## 63

Would you want your romantic partner to have a close friendship with a previous lover?

## 64

Your son loves science, and wants to join the science club at school, but he is worried that he will be teased by students not in the club.

What will you tell him to do?

65

Name five athletes you would "invite to the BBQ".

## 66

What is your favorite Kwanzaa principle?

Why?

## 67

A young Black man is killed by a police officer. Your friends want to go out and "rip stuff up". They expect you to join them.

Will you?

## 68

Do you have a relative whom you would be reluctant to invite to an important event for fear their personality would embarrass you or other family members?

## 69

You colleague at work wants a one night stand with a Black woman because he thinks the experience would be exciting. The colleague targets a friend of yours and asks for your help in setting up a date. He pretends as if he's interested in a relationship, but he doesn't know you know he just wants to hook up.

Would you help?

If the colleague was a woman seeking a man, would you help?

## 70

You learn of a City plan to relocate the tenants of a low-income "Project home" to a new single-family housing development.

The new housing development is near your home.

Would you favor or oppose the move?

## 71

If you were suddenly required to move out of your home for an extended time, where would you go?

**72**

While channel surfing, you come across a program where a Black person in the audience tells a very depressing tale of financial and health related challenges.   The person then claims to still have faith that things will improve.

Do you know someone who expresses this type of faith?

## 73

If you could, what would you say to the people in other countries who participated in supportive protests inspired by the killing of George Floyd?

## 74

While waiting with several non-Black friends for a table at a popular restaurant, a Black customer comes in and begins to speak to the wait staff in a rude, disrespectful and loud manner. The customer then leaves. Several other people in the restaurant then look at your group in a disapproving manner.

About what are they thinking?

What would you do?

## 75

While visiting your niece's home, you agree to take her to her softball league opening day game.   While waiting in line at the concession stand, you overhear some parents discussing names for a youth team's new mascot.   They appear to agree on the name "'Bush Babies."

What would you do?

## 76

Do you shake a Black person's hand differently than a non-Black person's hand?

## 77

Do you have a friend with a name from an African language?

Can you pronounce the name?

Do you know what does it mean?

## 78

What activity did you stop because of the COVID-19 quarantine and now, don't miss anymore?

## 79

It's your Birthday!   Your friends submitted your name to have a surprise dinner with your favorite celebrity.

And They Won!

So – you are going out with…?

80

While shopping at a store, you overhear customers discussing a community meeting where members plan to ask elected officials to support a "Stand Your Ground" law in your city.   The meeting is tonight.

Will you go?

## 81

Your uncle refuses to get a flu shot because he believes the government is experimenting on people. His wife tells you that his doctor strongly recommended the shot, and she asks you to convince your uncle to get the shot.

Would you?

## 82

Your friend is charged with a crime and pleads not guilty.  When you go to the trial, the jury walks in and everyone is White.

Will your friend get a fair trial?

## 83

Your grandfather invites you to a Juneteenth celebration at a local church. Your brother does not want to go because it is an "old, outdated holiday".

What do you do?

## 84

A non-Black actor announces on social media that she is staring in a new movie adaptation of a popular book, but in the book, the character is a successful, educated Black woman. Are you excited to see the movie, or will you pass?

85

You give a new friend a ride for a night out. When inside the car, your friend begins to change your radio station and the radio volume.

How do you respond?

## 86

Do you know someone whom you would trust to repair or "look at" your car or a nonworking appliance in your home?

## 87

You move to a new state, and need to choose a new attorney, doctor and dentist. When asking your new Black neighbor for advice, she says she never uses Black professionals.

What would you do?

88

Your friend's sister believes she has Black people in her family "because she has a wide nose." Do you agree with her?

89

Do you agree or disagree with this statement: Public school systems should strive to understand "Black English" or Ebonics, so that they can better communicate with Black youth.

Why?

## 90

Do you think it is appropriate for a person to get some benefit, such as a job or school enrollment, only because they are related to someone who makes a decision in their favor?

## 91

A member of a non-profit organization asks you to support a resolution that would increase your state taxes by $5 a year to create a fund to assist low-income people in the State. The resolution calls for a non-profit organization to administer the money. The local newspaper writes an Editorial in support, but local elected officials want a State agency to manage the program.

Would you support the tax increase?

If yes, who should manage the program – the non-profit organization or the State agency?

## 92

A non-Black person you meet at a friend's party greets you in a friendly manner, and says, "What up, my N***a?"

What is your response?

## 93

After a long week of work, you are looking forward to a relaxing weekend at home. It's Friday afternoon, and your cousin calls you and invites you to a surprise party for a dear elderly family member at his house later that evening. Meanwhile, you receive a text from your friend inviting you out to grand opening of a new club that night.

Both events are on the same night.

Where are you going?

94

What five musicians would you "invite to the BBQ"?

95

You decide to enroll in a class on Black History. When you review the course offerings, you discover that a White person teaches the class you want to take.

Will you take the course?

## 96

## Killmonger or Black Panther?

## 97

A new soul food restaurant opens in your neighborhood called *Brothaman's Chicken and Biscuits*.   It is not Black owned and no Black people work there.   Your uncle refuses to eat there "because it isn't *real* soul food", but your friend wants to try it out.

Will you eat there?

## 98

Do you believe there is a "Black Twitter"?

99

Your child wants to play a new video game that lets you create your own avatar as a character.  When you look at the instructions, you see that the design options are limited for people with darker complexions.

What would you tell your child?

## 100

You discover that the person you have been dating commits illegal acts for income.  Now the person wants to become "serious", but does not know that you know about the illegal activity.

What would you do?

101

Do you read Black owned media outlets?

Which one?

## 102

If you were a slave and could choose, would you prefer to work in the House or in the Field?

## 103

Your good friend is thinking about going out with a person they met on the Internet.   The person lives in another country.   Your friend wants your advice.

What would you tell them to do?

## 104

Your dark skinned cousin calls you to tell you she will be in a new major movie.

What type of character do you think she will play?

## 105

Have you ever heard that police were searching for a suspect in a horrible crime, and hoped that the perpetrator of the crime was NOT a Black person?

Why?

You come home to find your child visibly upset.  The child admits to behaving very badly outside.  Moments later your elderly neighbor knocks on your door, points at your child and says "I saw what happened.  I got a switch from the tree and I whipped 'em good!"

What would you do?

## 107

A fast car just misses a woman crossing the street.   She looks at you and says, "I wish that car had hit me.   I would be rich if it had."

What would you say?

You move into a new apartment and upon connecting your television, you discover that the cable television/satellite service is still connected in the previous tenant's name.

Will you use the service?

109

Do you agree or disagree with the following statement:

Black law enforcement officials should be more lenient with Black suspects.

## 110

Do you support the Patient Protection and Affordable Care Act?

## 111

While waiting in line for a table at a restaurant with a few Black friends, you notice that several other groups as large as yours are seated before you, even though you have been waiting longer.

How would you respond?

## 112

What's your favorite Black website, app or social networking feed?

113

Your family is trying to decide where your very independent, but sick elderly relative will live.

Will you offer your home?

The Parent Teacher Association at your nephew's school wants to announce their support for a recommendation to allow teachers to carry loaded weapons in class.

Would you support the recommendation?

## 115

A police officer in your neighborhood shoots a Black person. Rumors suggest that the victim was shot while in a defenseless position, but law enforcement officials claim that the victim had a weapon.

What would you expect the Mayor to say at the press conference?

## 116

You and your six-year-old nephew visit your friend's house.  The teenager of the house is getting ready to meet his friends.  You notice that his pants are clearly "sagging" when he leaves.  Your nephew sees him walk out and immediately looks at you.

What would you say to your nephew?

## 117

When applying for college, you receive admission to two schools. School "A" offers enrollment through a special "Minority enrollment program" based solely on your race. There, you will receive various counseling and you will be enrolled in an internship program. School "B" does not have a Minority enrollment program. Instead, "B" offers you unqualified admission with no extra assistance beyond what is offered to all other students.

Would you accept the offer for enrollment from school "A" or "B"?

## 118

Do you believe H.I.V is man-made?

## 119

What's your favorite International TV or streaming show?

Does it bother you to see two Black people of the same gender in a romantic relationship with each other?

Why or why not?

## 121

While eating lunch with three Black colleagues, a White colleague comes over and says, "I'm going to sit at the Black table".

What do you do?

# 122

# Is Black History Month still necessary?

## 123

You read two sports stories about a fight between players at a hockey and basketball game.

What will the media say about the fights?

## 124

Describe one of your favorite viral videos.

What makes it your favorite?

## 125

While walking through your friend's apartment building, you smell some food cooking from a nearby apartment. Your friend tells you the neighbor is from the Caribbean, and would invite you in to try the dish if asked.

Would you ask?

## 126

A friend approaches you and asks you to volunteer as a donor so that they can have a child.

What would the friend have to say for you to agree?

## 127

Your nephew is going for a job interview. He needs to spend some time researching for the position, get a new pair of shoes, a haircut and shave, and a go to the dentist for a cleaning. Unfortunately, he only has time for three of the tasks.

Which task should he skip?

You receive two invitations for parties the same evening.  One will have an open bar while friendly people who do not drink host the other.

Which would you attend?

## 129

You are crossing the street when you see a woman approaching from the opposite sidewalk.   As you approach, she shifts her purse to the side of her body that is opposite of you.

Does this bother you?

## 130

If you were suddenly unable to care for your children, what qualities would you want in your child's new family?

## 131

Do you know all of the words and the melody to the Black National Anthem "Lift Every Voice and Sing"?

Can you sing it now?

## 132

You go out to dinner on a blind date. When your bill for your evening arrives, your date says "excuse me for a moment", and walks out. Moments later, you see your date outside, waiving wildly and encouraging you to leave the restaurant without paying.

Would you go?

133

After conviction of a crime, your romantic partner must serve at least 7 years in prison.

Will you wait to continue the relationship after they have served their time or move on?

## 134

When leaving for work one morning, you find a flier on your car encouraging people in your neighborhood to join a racist organization.

How would you respond?

135

How did you get a copy of these questions?

## 136

One of your friends invites you to "Friends and Family Day" at their church.  As a visiting guest, the usher brings you a microphone, and the Pastor encourages you to introduce yourself to the congregation and share a few words.

What would you say?

## 137

Do you have an older relative or friend that sings while working?

What songs do they sing?

## 138

What historical event has had the greatest impact on Black people?

Why did you select that event?

## 139

When walking through the security sensors of a crowded store with a group of people, the security alarms sound.  A security guard quickly walks over to you and asks that you come to the back office so that he can check your bags.

How would you respond?

## 140

When your friend leaves the room, your friend's diabetic mother rushes to a kitchen cabinet and gets a carton of sugar. She then pours A LOT of sugar in her extra large cup of fruit punch. With a big smile, she says "Shhhhh" to you, asks you to keep her secret from your friend, and leaves.

What would you do?

## 141

If given the opportunity to visit Africa, would you go?

## 142

Name your favorite Black love story.

What do you like most about it?

## 143

A group promoting racist views requests permission to hold a rally in your neighborhood. The local government invites citizens to file comments on the application.

Will you file a comment?

## 144

You overhear an argument between your neighbor and her elderly father. They are debating the value of a college education for your neighbor's child. The neighbor says it is a bad idea because loans take years to pay off. The father says it is worth it. They notice you and ask your opinion.

What would you say?

## 145

After another relationship ends badly, your Black, young and financially stable friend decides to date non-Black people exclusively.

What advice would you give?

## 146

While visiting your friend's house, her 4th grade child comes home and begins to tell you about the day's lessons on the 1960's Civil Rights marches. The lesson focused on the peaceful intentions of the marches, but does not say anything about the violent response.

How would you respond to the child's story?

### 147

After returning from a rally against discrimination, you see pictures online of protesters wounded after clashing with law enforcement. Several of the people in the pictures are not Black.

If you could, what would you say to the non-Black protesters?

Do you think Black teachers are best able to teach Black children?

Why or why not?

## 149

Your friend Andre comes to town for a visit, and invites you and a few others out to dinner - and he's paying!   One of your friends brings empty containers because he plans to order extra food to bring home because, well, Andre's paying!   He asks you to bring some extra containers for him too.

Will you bring the extra containers?

## 150

When your friend's three year old child gets cranky, your friend gives her a tablet to play various games, sometimes for hours at a time. Some are learning games, some just waste time. Thanks to the tablet games, the child can count to 50, knows 16 colors and his ABC's. The child's Grandma thinks the tablet is a terrible idea because it is being used as a "babysitter". Grandma thinks the child needs discipline and personal attention instead and, that the tablet should be turned off.

They agree to let you settle the debate. What would you recommend?

## 151

While watching a music channel with your friends, one of them points at the screen excitedly and says "turn it up – that's my jam!"

Who do you think was on the screen?

## 152

You have decided to purchase a home. Your real estate broker recommends several areas with very high numbers of Black residents. The broker is very reluctant to show you homes in areas where Black people are not the majority because of concerns that you may not "fit in".

What would you do?

153

You discover that your lover is sexting with other people.

What would you do?

**154**

Do you take different safety precautions when traveling through predominately-Black neighborhoods?

## 155

Your six-year-old niece says she has a boyfriend.

How would you respond?

## 156

A young Black man runs up to your porch and asks you to help him.  He says a gang is chasing him right now, and if you do not help, they will catch and hurt him.

What would you do?

Your friend Chantey has an interview for a new job in an office setting. She is considering wearing her hair natural for the interview, but her Aunt says she should go "professional" and get a perm or weave.

Chantey asks for your advice.

What would you say?

158

Your nephew wants you to get him a pair of the latest sneakers for his birthday. The sneakers costs $175.

Will you purchase it for him?

Due to very high demand, you will have to wait in line for several hours at the mall.

Would you still purchase the sneaker?

## 159

If a grant was offered to open your own business, and it required only that you select a location, would you consider it a "business only" decision to select the location or would you feel obligated to open in a predominately-Black community?

## 160

An African nation announces the production of a new "made in Africa" automobile.

What would influence you to purchase the vehicle?

## 161

What's your favorite Blaxploitation film?

## 162

While crossing the street, a car drives by with music coming out of the window.   An intoxicated woman standing near you shouts "Aww that's Teddy!!!   That's my song!!!" She then starts singing the song.

She <u>cannot</u> sing to save her life.

What do you do?

163

What does your family do for fun when together?

## 164

After allegations of racist acts are made against your favorite fast food chain, people online call for a boycott.

Would you support the boycott and take your business elsewhere, or continue to support the business by ignoring the boycott?

165

Name your favorite hip hop artist.

## 166

You go to a concert and discover that someone is sitting in your seats.

How do you respond?

## 167

Your friend's brother Anthony is thinking about asking a lovely young woman out on a date, but he is reluctant because she does not have "a lot to twerk with".

What advice would you give Anthony?

## 168

Your childhood friend Leroy wants to go on a date with a woman who told him she hates her father.  She says she does not know anyone in a happy relationship.

What advice would you give Leroy?

## 169

Your colleague from work needs to get three gifts for Valentine's Day.   One for a spouse, and two for "sides".   You are asked for your advice on what type of gift to get.

How would you respond?

After the gifts are given, you realize that one of your friends received a gift from your colleague.   Your friend is unaware of their "side status".

What would you do?

## 170

Your friend invites you to a UniverSoul Circus™ performance. Your OTHER friend invites you to see the Alvin Ailey Dance Ensemble™. Your cousin then asks if you would like to go see Hamilton™ on tour. Each performance is on the same day.

Which performance would you go see?

171

You go to a store that sells hair care products for Black people.   When you go in, you see that no one Black works there.

Will you still shop there?

## 172

Do you believe that you will find or are currently in a relationship with a "good Black man or woman"?

# 173

## Do you talk about Black issues with people who are not Black?

You attend a ceremony sponsored by a Black organization.  During acceptance remarks, one of the award recipients expresses appreciation and love for a spouse.  The spouse comes on stage, and is not Black.

What is your first reaction?

## 175

## Supremes, En Vogue, or Destiny's Child?

## 176

What five actors would get an "invite to the BBQ"?

## 177

Would you be proud to be the first Black person to achieve a certain distinction?

## 178

While at a car dealer to get some new rims and a new stereo installed, your friend tells you that the mechanic suggests he get new brakes too.   Your friend can only afford two upgrades.

Which would you recommend?

## 179

Your friend says she does not vote because she does not want to get jury duty.

What would you tell her?

180

God appears on Earth as a dark skinned Black man with a big Afro.

How will the world react?

## 181

After two children and seven years of marriage, your best friend is considering having an affair.

What would you tell your friend to do?

## 182

To avoid a sudden storm, you decide to catch the bus. Two seats are available when you get on board—one next to an elderly White man, the other next to a Black man wearing a hoodie.

Where do you sit?

183

Your romantic partner expresses an interest in exploring various sexual acts unrecognizable to you.

What would you do?

## 184

Of all Black men you know personally, name three good qualities that they have in common.

185

Would you want to work for a corporation that has a reputation for racist hiring practices?

## 186

Finish this sentence: Yo Mama is sooo_____.

187

You have been invited to a 70's party. What would you wear?

188

Of your favorite books, which was the last that you shared with another person?

It's OK if this is your new favorite book…

;-)

## 189

Your friend asks you to join her at a custody hearing for her child.   She is worried because her ex is bringing his crazy, "ratchet" friend Big Bae to the hearing.

Will you go?

190

A colleague at your new job tells you that your predecessor in the same position was Black.

Would this information bother you?

# 191

Can a woman raise a boy to be a man?

192

Aside from showing you a picture, how could someone you do not know and cannot see prove to you that they are Black?

## 193

While completing an application to join an organization, your friend's son asks you to help him choose a category for race. Your friend's son has a Black parent and a White parent.

What would you tell him?

## 194

Your daughter comes home from High School and announces that he wants to join the military.  Your mother-in-law thinks this is a wonderful choice, while your mother is strongly opposed and thinks she should go to a regular college.

What do you say?

## 195

You get a call from a company that claims you have won half a million dollars. They seem to know everything about you. To send you the money you must give them a checking account number for direct deposit.

Will you give them the information?

The DJ for your birthday party asks you to choose your favorite party anthem.

What song do you choose?

197

Do you believe Black people have opportunities for a good life in America?

Your uncle Ray Ray tells you he is getting into the business of selling life insurance.   He wants you to buy a policy from him.

Will you?

What would a friend or family member have to do to get your financial support for a new business?

## 199

When should a government be allowed to conduct surveillance on its citizens?

If you were alive in the 1960's, would you have supported the political strategies of the Rev. Dr. Martin Luther King Jr., or El-Hajj Malik El-Shabazz?

Why?

## 201

You win two tickets to attend a Black museum or Art gallery.  You get to choose the location.

Where would you go? Why?

## 202

If you were a slave and heard about a plan to escape, would you risk death and run for your freedom or would you stay and work to earn your freedom?

203

While riding in an elevator an elderly White woman comes in. Moments later her cellphone starts ringing and the ringtone is *"Fight the Power"* by Public Enemy.

How would you respond?

## 204

You speak with a reporter covering a story about a Black athlete's community involvement day with 200 elementary school students. Later that evening, you hear that there have been three murders in the city.

Which story will lead the evening news?

## 205

Should President Obama comment publicly on issues that directly affect the Black community?

## 206

You are asked to join a committee working to organize a Black Family Festival. What activities would you want to see there?

207

Do you believe that more Black shows should be on television?

How many?

208

You are the only Black person in attendance at a program discussing political issues.  At one point, another participant suggests that you respond "on behalf of Black people".

How would you respond?

## 209

Have you ever given or received a "shout out" on a radio station?

210

You receive a large, unexpected bill from a collection company.

What's the first thing you'll do?

## 211

## Sheneneh, Wanda or Madea?

## 212

Have you named certain "parts" of your body?

# 213

# Did O.J. do it?

## 214

Your friend asks you to join a Black gun owner organization.

What would you say?

## 215

One morning you wake up and discover that all Black people are living together on a new world far from Earth. We cannot go back to Earth.

Describe our New World.

Now describe Earth.

You receive an invitation from a new colleague at work to attend an evening event sponsored by a Nigerian organization.  You are told that you can bring a friend.

Would you go?

Would you bring a friend?

## 217

You get to plan a romantic evening at your home. What song is playing in the background when you open the door to welcome your guest?

## 218

Do you have a secret you have kept from a family member or loved one? If yes, has any good come from your secrecy?

## 219

What is the single greatest problem facing the Black community today?

When was the last time you had a dentist or doctor's appointment?

What were the results?

221

Would you be comfortable working in an office where all of the staff are Black?

## 222

You are describing an attractive person to a close friend.

What words would you use?

## 223

You suspect that your friends Dennis and Layla are trying to set you up on a date. They have asked you to describe your perfect evening.

What would you tell them?

## 224

Your friend wants to name her daughter Influenza because she met the father while getting a Flu vaccination. She asks you for your opinion.

What advice would you give?

## 225

Should Rap and Hip Hop artists get inducted into the Rock and Roll Hall of Fame?

## 226

Where is the best place to live in America for Black people?

## 227

## What should you expect to happen at a funeral for a Black person?

## 228

## Magic, Air Jordan, Black Mamba or King James?

## 229

While listening to a radio show, you hear a caller complain about losing a promotion to a Black person. The caller believes the Employer promoted the Black person because of race.

Do you think this happens?

Your friend invites you to exercise at the local gym. When you leave the locker room, you overhear several people criticizing a Black person's clothing as too revealing because Black people "can't wear those types of clothes in public".

What would you do?

## 231

You visit your friend's house for the weekend, and join her at a small high school basketball game.  Since you do not know the players, you listen to the local broadcast of the game while sitting in the stands.  After watching a Black athlete aggressively block the shot of a White player, the announcer says "those boys are just naturally gifted athletes."

What would you do?

232

Your child is excited to get one of a series of new Black action figure toys.  When the toys become available, each of them has typical Black features, but they have blue eyes.

What would you do?

## 233

Your friend Linay is angry and upset because she was blocked on social media by her young daughter.

Linay wants to confront her daughter, and asks you for advice.

What will you say?

Your nephew is upset about news stories about the federal government's treatment of undocumented immigrants.  He asks you what you think should happen.

What would you say?

## 235

Your child's class decides to make a time capsule.  Everyone is invited to put something in it.  Your child asks you to give them something to put in the capsule.

What would you give your child?

## 236

## Would you pass a "Paper Bag Test"?

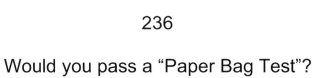

## 237

Who is your favorite fictional character?

## 238

If you could change one thing about yourself, what would it be?

If changing that one thing meant losing something else you like about yourself, would it be worth it?

If so, what would you lose?

## 239

While checking out at a local store, an elderly lady in front of you is one dollar short for her purchase of milk and bread.   She looks at you, but doesn't ask you for the difference.

Will you give her the money she needs?

## 240

Would you allow unrelated victims of a major storm to move into your home for an extended period?

## 241

Are you offended when non-Black people receive awards at Black ceremonies?

## 242

While kneeling at a store to get an item off a low shelf, you notice a little boy staring at you. While his mother stands nearby looking at other products, the boy walks over and asks if he can touch your hair.

His mother looks over and just smiles at you.

What would you say?

## 243

While chaperoning a pajama party for your friend's nine year old son and friends, you overhear one of the boys discussing the finer parts of a woman's' body.

How would you respond?

## 244

A friend's gravely ill parent wants to give you authority to stop all attempts to save her life if no hope remains.   She does not want her family to make the final decision, including your friend.

Would you accept the responsibility?

## 245

While your friend is upstairs, you overhear her 19-year-old son set up a date with his new "girlfriend". Your friend does not know the girlfriend, but you recognize the woman's name as a neighbor who happens to be *at least* 40 years old.

How would you respond?

A Black person is shot. Rumors suggest the shooter is Black.

What type of community reaction would you expect?

If the victim were your loved one, what would you want the community to do?

## 247

What would your grandparents do if you were walking down the street and you were about to "split a pole"?

## 248

Have you ever seen someone "catch the Holy Ghost"?

What happened?

## 249

Your uncle stops by your home with a bag of clothes he picked up from an organization that accepts clothing donations for needy people. He tells you picked them out for you.

What would you do?

## 250

Your friend Angie's mentally disabled cousin is visiting for the weekend.  She wants to hang out with you, and bring him over so that he can play with your nephew.  Your friend says you should say "no", because he believes the child's mental disability will "rub off" onto your nephew.

What would you say to Angie?

## 251

As you get in the elevator, a person you know walks out.   The remaining two people you do not know start talking badly about the person that just exited the elevator.

What would you do?

252

A White colleague at work accidently sends you an email you immediately determine to be racist humor directed at Black people.

What would you do?

## 253

Would you accept a job at the White House?

254

Who is your favorite author?

## 255

While walking down the street, you see a group of Black children playing cops and robbers. Two of them are using toy guns that look somewhat real. Two blocks up the street, you notice a police car turning the corner. It's driving down the street towards the children.

What would you do?

Your thirteen-year-old niece spends a few weeks during her summer break with you. You decide to go shopping. She calls out from another room and says she is ready to go, and then comes out dressed in very revealing clothing.

How would you respond?

## 257

What do you do to stop the "Itis"?

258

Who is your ride or die?

How did they earn that respect?

259

Your friend is considering applying for a promotion at work, but is concerned the supervisor will want to spend the evening together so that it can be "earned".

What would you suggest?

260

Name a product or service that is produced by Black people and is purchased by all people.

261

Since the events surrounding the Rodney King incident in 1991, what steps has the Black community taken to prevent similar occurrences in the future.

What steps should be taken?

## 262

Your Black friend asks you to come with him to look at a new house for sale. It is late in the afternoon when you both arrive, and the sales agent says she is on the way. So, you decide to wait in the car. While waiting, several people watch you from their windows. Then, one of them walk over and ask why you are sitting there. They also ask for identification. Your friend is outraged! He loudly tells the person to mind his business. Suddenly three other people start walking over to the car. Your friend then asks if you "have his back".

What do you say?

## 263

Your son comes home from the barber with a crooked hairline.

What would you do?

264

Your friend wants to buy a new car.  You ask her if she has checked her FICO score.  She laughs at you and says "Um yeah, whatever. I got something for FICO...".

What advice would you give to your friend?

265

While walking in the mall, you see a group of teenagers whispering and looking at you. You look away, then look back and immediately notice that one used his cell phone to take your picture.

What would you do?

266

You receive a call from Mr. Smith, a collection agent.  Mr. Smith is looking for one of your friends, and he asks if you will provide contact information.

You say...:

While out at a celebration, a close friend has several alcoholic drinks and begins to express intense romantic feelings towards you. Later that evening, the friend invites you to take them home and spend the night.

Together.

Would you go?

During a traditional pouring of libations ceremony, participants are invited to honor deceased ancestors, related and not, and embrace their wisdom by calling their name.

When it begins, what names do you call out?

You lose a bet to your friends, and have to perform a karaoke song from the music they choose.   The music options are:

K-Pop;
Afro Pop;
Reggaeton; or
Metal.

What music type will you pick?

## 270

After losing a double or nothing bet, your friends challenge your dancing skills.  They choose the style. Your choices are:

Samba;
Break dancing;
Soca;
Line dancing; or
freestyle!

Which dance type would you perform?

Um, what are you waiting for…?

## 271

Your friend asks you if she can use your mailing address to have some expensive items delivered because she is afraid they may be stolen if delivered to her home.

What would you tell her?

272

Your friend invites you to a New Year's Eve watch night.  What type of event are you expecting?  Where will you go?

## 273

Your friend loses her job and decides to apply for a private financial assistance program. The program promises to give approved applicants a free grant, but collects a range of personally identifiable information such as fingerprints, photos, the child's social security number, address, and a background check. Your friend is concerned that the program is collecting a lot of personal information. She asks for your advice.

What would you tell her?

© 2014, 2020 Odogwu O. Linton, Esq.   All Rights Reserved.

## 274

While visiting your friend's home, you leave your phone unlocked on a chair and go to the restroom. Your friend walks into the room and hears your phone beeping. She picks it up, and sees the final text messages your ex sent you.

What will your friend think of you?

## 275

Do you believe the American government is participating in a conspiracy to prevent Black people from advancing in American society?

## 276

When you were growing up, what phrase or comment would an adult use to let you know they have had enough of your bad behavior?

## 277

Have you attempted to trace your ancestry? How far can you go back through your family tree? Did you find any surprises?

## 278

The manager at your local fitness center tells you that a gym bag was reported stolen by someone who "looks like a Black person". The manager would like to get every Black person in the gym to come to his office for a "quick line up", to see if the accuser can identify the thief. The manager thinks it will be easy, since there are only six Black people in the gym and "if they're innocent, they have nothing to hide".

Do you agree with the Manager?

What would you say?

## 279

You find out that your child's elementary school teacher refuses to adhere to a new zero tolerance anti-discrimination policy.

What would you do?

Your employer asks you to sit on a committee to develop an anti-discrimination company policy. When you attend the meeting, you notice that only Black women are in the room.

Describe what you think the policy will say.

While sitting in your car at a red light, a young boy comes to your window and asks for a donation to a local sports team.   No adults appear to be in the area.


What would you do?

One of your online friends tells you that she wants to leave social media for a while because she is tired of "racist trolls attacking her posts".

What would you tell her to do?

283

What's the first thing you would do with a Tubman dollar bill?

## 284

You win backstage concert access for you and three friends to see your favorite singer! When you arrive, other winners are in the waiting area waiting for the musicians to come out of their dressing rooms. While waiting, you overhear a member of the stage crew commenting that the singers will pay less attention to the white fans because they prefer "Chocolate skin, not Vanilla skin".

Two of your friends are "Vanilla".

What would you do?

Choose one:

Horrible smelling lotion

Or

Ashy hands

What nickname did one of your friends or family members have as a child that does not really fit anymore, but everyone uses it anyway?

Your friend wants to travel to another country, but does not know where she wants to go. What factors would influence your choice to go to one country over another?

## 288

When a new documentary about Black history is announced on social media, a person on the site posts a comment asking why there is not a similar documentary about White history.

What would you say in response?

## 289

Describe the last product or service you obtained from a Black owned business.

Choose One:

aspireTV;
BET;
BounceTV;
TV One;
OWN: the Oprah Winfrey Network

## 291

Describe the qualities you want in a person you call "friend."

Do you have people in your life that you refer to as friend, but they do not match the qualities you have listed?

## 292

A large storm knocks our power to your home. What do you do to pass the time?

Are you waiting for the power restoration, or can you stay home without it?

## 293

When the COVID – 19 stay at home orders were issued, what were the top five items you had to have in your home?

Were you able to get them?

Would women or men who know you define you as a "good Black woman" or a "good Black man"?

295

Describe the last celestial event that you watched. What was special about it?

Your colleague at work tells you that he wants to get a dog that can protect his home from anyone that comes on his property, especially Black people.

What would you say?

## 297

Your third grade child tells you that another child at school has been calling Black children "bad names". When your child tells you one of the names, you interpret it as a racial slur.

How would you respond?

## 298

Should America legalize illegal drugs?

299

Do you enjoy any foods or music that would surprise your friends if they found out about it?

300

Which question is your favorite?

Tell us online at:

#ConversateTheBook
#ConversateHotNumber

© 2014, 2020 Odogwu O. Linton, Esq.   All Rights Reserved.